SPIRITUAL ADVICE
FOR BUDDHISTS AND CHRISTIANS

HIS HOLINESS THE DALAI LAMA

Spiritual Advice for Buddhists and Christians

EDITED BY
DONALD W. MITCHELL

Continuum • New York

1998
The Continuum Publishing Company
370 Lexington Avenue
New York, NY 10017

Copyright © 1998 by Monastic Interreligious Dialogue

Printed in the United States of America

Library of Congress Cataloging-in-Publication Data

Bstan-`dzin-rgya-mtsho, Dalai Lama XIV, 1935–   .
    Spiritual advice for Buddhists and Christians / His Holiness
the Dalai Lama : edited by Donald W. Mitchell.
        p.   cm.
    ISBN 0-8264-1076-6
    1. Spiritual life—Buddhism. 2. Spiritual life—Christianity.
I. Mitchell, Donald W. (Donald William), 1943–   .   II. Title.
BQ7935.B774S65   1998
294.3`444—dc21   98-16984
                                                          CIP

Contents

Preface

Thirty years ago, Thomas Merton traveled to Bangkok to attend the very first East–West intermonastic conference called by the world's Benedictine abbots. Prior to that conference, Thomas Merton met with His Holiness the Dalai Lama in what was for both men a profound experience of spiritual friendship. Then in Bangkok, just after delivering his presentation on the second day of the intermonastic conference, Thomas Merton suddenly died. That conference and the death of Thomas Merton marked the birth of a new and fascinating spiritual encounter between the great traditions of Buddhist and Christian spiritualities.

In 1977, almost ten years after Merton's death, the Benedictine tradition established a formal organization, named Monastic Interreligious Dialogue (MID), to stimulate, develop, and assist in exchanges and dialogues especially between Buddhist and Christian monastics from the West and the East. With this support, the 1980s and 1990s were years in which numerous Zen and Tibetan monastics—both monks and nuns—traveled to Christian monasteries in Europe and America, while many Christian monks and nuns traveled to Zen and Tibetan monasteries in Asia.

Christians survived harrowing jeep rides, monsoons, landslides, mountain lions, giant spiders, and hungry mice to venture to ancient monasteries in remote parts of Asia. Buddhists also traveled to far-away monastic sites like Montserrat, Spain, where they climbed mountain peaks to visit Christian hermits. Wherever the exchange took place—in the peaceful rooms of Zen monasteries in Kyoto, Tibetan nunneries in Dharamsala, or Christian convents in New Mexico—the internal dialogue of the heart opened new vistas of spiritual life to visitors and hosts alike. Gradually, a new level of trust and respect developed from the mutual understanding and appreciation that emerged from these exchanges. In the context of this deeper spiritual friendship, more practical issues were also addressed.

For example, MID has been helping their Tibetan brothers and sisters gain the health care expertise, computer skills, and educational proficiency they need to serve better their people in exile.

It was based on this decades-long friendship that in 1993 His Holiness the Dalai Lama attended a MID inter-monastic dialogue at the Parliament of the World's Religions in Chicago. After this formal encounter, His Holiness said that he felt the ground was prepared well enough for an in-depth dialogue on the spiritual life. He suggested that twenty-five Buddhist and twenty-five Christian spiritual teachers and practitioners live together, meditate and pray together, and hold a dialogue with each other about spirituality and its value in today's world. His Holiness also asked if the encounter might be held at the Abbey of Gethsemani, the home of his dear friend Thomas Merton. While intermonastic exchanges and dialogues had been taking place during the past thirty years, this would be the first such event held at a global level of encounter.

MID followed up on this suggestion of His Holiness, and during July 1996 the now famous and historic Gethsemani Encounter was held. Besides His

Holiness the Dalai Lama, Buddhist monastics and lay practitioners attended from Theravada, Tibetan, and Zen traditions in Sri Lanka, Thailand, Myanmar, Cambodia, Taiwan, Korea, Japan, India, and throughout the United States. On the Christian side, monastics from the Benedictine and Trappist orders, as well as lay practitioners, attended from Europe, Asia, North America, and Australia. The topics that were discussed in the dialogues were (1) the practice of prayer and meditation in the spiritual life, (2) the stages of growth in the process of spiritual development, (3) the role of the teacher and the community in the spiritual life, and (4) the goals of spiritual and social transformation.

In order to share the spiritual fruits of this historic event, a beautiful book has been published with all of the spiritual talks by Buddhist and Christian masters. Also included in that book is an edited version of the actual dialogue about such important issues as the nature of the mind, overcoming anger, love and compassion, the use of scripture, mystical experience, the dynamics of grace and blessings, discernment of spirits, addressing violence and social injustice, the meaning of suffering, and building unity in a divided world. The book is entitled: *The Gethsemani Encounter: A Dialogue on the Spiritual Life by Buddhist and Christian Monastics,* edited by Donald W. Mitchell and James Wiseman, O.S.B. (New York: Continuum, 1997).

All of the talks presented at the Gethsemani Encounter on Tibetan Buddhist spirituality were given by His Holiness the Dalai Lama. When as editors of *The Gethsemani Encounter* we prepared these talks for publication, we were happily surprised to see that they included many words of advice directed to Christians as well as Buddhists. So, what you have in your hands now is the spiritual advice that His Holiness gave in those talks and in his dialogue with both Buddhists and Christians at the Gethsemani Encounter.

In chapter 1, His Holiness speaks about how religions are like medicines healing humanity and can contribute through interfaith dialogue to building a more peaceful and united world. In chapter 2, he goes on to discuss how the inner journey of meditation can heal our afflictive emotions and bring us peace and happiness. In chapter 3, His Holiness gives us suggestions concerning the process of reaching "calm abiding" through confronting such ills as low self-esteem, laziness, and self-doubt in ways that can be helpful to Christians as well as Buddhists. In chapter 4, he discusses and gives advice about such qualities of the spiritual life as charity, love, and compassion; he also explains the nature of wisdom from the Buddhist point of view. In chapter 5, His Holiness describes the characteristics of the spiritual guide that one should look for in choosing a religious teacher. Finally, in chapter 6, His Holiness presents the Buddhist goal of overcoming ignorance, finding the mind of clear light, and attaining Nirvana. He recognizes the difference between this attainment and the Christian ideal of union with God, and goes on to suggest a spiritual goal for all humankind, namely, to cultivate "the positive human qualities of tolerance, generosity, and love."

I would like to thank the following for their support and assistance in preparing this volume: MID, the Office of Tibet, the Abbey of Gethsemani, Sr. Mary Margaret Funk, Fr. James Wiseman, Gene Gollogly, Frank Oveis, Doris Cross, Jeffrey Hopkins, Kristen Mitchell, and of course most especially His Holiness the Dalai Lama.

Donald W. Mitchell

· 1 ·

The
Journey
of
Dialogue

$\mathcal{T}$he need for spirituality is obvious. I think so long as there are human beings, some kind of spirituality is necessary. It may not be necessary for all human beings, but at least for millions of human beings. Therefore, there is today a very great interest in spirituality.

religion as medicine

$\mathcal{N}$ow, it is also quite clear that different religious traditions—in spite of having different philosophies and viewpoints—all have a spiritual potential to help humanity by promoting human happiness and satisfaction. As a matter of fact, given the vast array of humanity

—of so many different kinds of people, of so many people with differing mental dispositions—we need a variety of religious traditions and so it is far better to have this variety.

Religions are like medicine in that the important thing is to cure human suffering. In the practice of medicine, it is not a question of how expensive the medicine is; what is important is to cure the illness in a particular patient. Similarly, you see, there is a variety of religions with their different philosophies and traditions. The aim or purpose of each religion is to cure the pains and unhappiness of the human mind. Here too, it is not a question of which religion is superior as such. The question is, which will better cure a particular person.

As a Buddhist monk, a Buddhist practitioner, from my own Buddhist tradition I have learned the importance of the suitability of religion according to an individual's mental disposition. For example, in what we call Mahayana Buddhism, the *bodhisattvayana*, there are different views about reality. Each school's interpretation is based on Shakyamuni Buddha's own words as recorded in certain sutras.

So it may seem that the one teacher, Shakyamuni Buddha, himself creates contradictions for his own followers. This is certainly not due to his own confusion concerning his own viewpoint. Certainly not. We believe that Shakyamuni Buddha is enlightened, in full realization of the truth. Therefore, we must conclude that he deliberately taught different philosophies according to the different mental dispositions of his followers. So from just our own tradition, we can learn about how important a person's mental disposition is for determining which religious tradition is best for him or her. It is not a question of determining that one interpretation of reality is true, and that since another is false you therefore should follow this first interpretation. You cannot say that. Even Buddha could not say that.

Therefore, from this experience it becomes very clear that for certain people a Christian method is much more effective than others. Muslims find their own approach to better suit their lives. So we cannot say, "this religion is good, that religion is not good." That we cannot say.

On an individual basis, however, we can say that a particular religion is best for us. For example, the

Buddhist way is best for me. There is no doubt! But this does not mean that Buddhism is best for everyone. And even within Buddhism, Madhyamika philosophy is best for me. But I cannot say that this view is best for all Buddhists. We cannot say that! So it is on this basis that it is extremely important to appreciate all the different religious traditions of the world, and particularly the major world religions. I think that there are sufficient reasons to respect and appreciate all the major world religious traditions.

It seems to me that we can divide humanity into three groups. One group—which is the majority—has no interest in religion. These persons are simply concerned about daily life—especially about money. Then there is another group which has a very sincere religious faith and practices some type of religion. Finally, the third group is intentionally very much opposed to any religious ideas. Looking at these three groups, we see that they are all the same in one regard: they all seek happiness. Here, there is no difference.

But differences do arise concerning how to achieve happiness. The first group believes that money alone can bring happiness. The second believes that it is through religious spirituality that we can attain happiness. And the third group believes not only that we benefit from money, but also that religious ideas are actually very poisonous to human happiness. They believe that religion is used by the ruling class of older societies as an instrument to exploit the masses. During much of this century, there has been competition between this antireligious group and religions. Recently, however, it seems that the value of religion for human happiness is becoming clearer to more and more people.

a constructive competition

While religions do promote human happiness, at the same time it is also clear that in the name of religious traditions there are more divisions among humanity, and in some cases even conflict and bloodshed. Not only in the past, but even today this is happening. This is very, very unfortunate! On the one hand, there is still the healing value of religious traditions. But on the other hand, sometimes unfortunate things happen due to these same religious traditions. So the choice must be made to maintain religious traditions while trying to minimize conflicts due to different contemporary situations.

In this regard, I always tell audiences that interfaith dialogue can improve closer understanding between different religious traditions. One type of dialogue involves scholars meeting in a more academic way to clarify the differences and similarities between their traditions. This type of dialogue provides a valuable way to help people understand and appreciate each other's religions and build bridges between different religious communities.

A second way of dialogue is pilgrimage by followers of different religious traditions. They can go together as a group in order to make a pilgrimage to the holy places of different religious traditions. The pilgrims should pray together if possible; if not, they can practice silent meditation. This is a very effective way to understand the value and power of other religious traditions. I personally have gone on such pilgrimages. For example, as a Buddhist I have no particular connection with Jerusalem. But, because I believe that all religious traditions have great potential, with that belief I visited Jerusalem as a pilgrim.

A third kind of dialogue is a meeting like the "Day of Prayer for Peace" in Assisi in 1986. While there, religious leaders came together and exchanged a few nice words. That was also very helpful. In the eyes of millions of people, it was very, very helpful. That kind of event eventually creates a more positive grass-roots atmosphere wherein religious leaders can then discuss various crucial matters.

A fourth type of dialogue involves a meeting between genuine practitioners of different religious traditions. This is to me very, very important; very, very helpful. An example was my meeting with the late Thomas Merton. Also at the Gethsemani Encounter, there was a long discussion about how to face anger. That part of the discussion I really felt was a clear example of spiritual dialogue. The Christian practitioners and the Buddhist practitioners both realize that anger is something negative. We both have to work on the problem of anger, even if our methods are different. Christians have a faith in God, and through that way they try to work on the problem. Buddhists have another way. But it has the same objective, the same purpose.

I also think that besides our dialogues we should have a kind of constructive competition. Buddhists should implement what we believe in daily life, and our Christian brothers and sisters should also implement their teachings in daily life. So on that field, I think, we should have some competition. Since each side would like to be better practitioners, there is no harm in such competition—it is really constructive. On the other hand, to say that my practice is better than another's, I do not think that is of much use. So that is my basic belief, my basic feeling, about the encounter of our religious traditions.

thomas merton

*A*s a result of meeting and dialogues with Thomas Merton, my attitude toward Christianity was greatly changed and very much improved. I always consider him a strong bridge between Buddhism and Christianity. From the point of view of a religious practitioner, and in particular as a monastic, Thomas

Merton really is someone that we can all look up to. From one point of view, he had the complete qualities of hearing—which means study, contemplating, thinking on the teachings—and of meditation. He also had the qualities of being learned, disciplined, and having a good heart. He not only was able to practice himself, but his perspective was very, very broad.

It seems to me that we should seek to follow the example that he gave to us. In this way, even though the chapter of his life is over, what he was hoping and seeking to do can remain forever. It seems to me that if all of us follow his model, it would be of very great benefit to the world.

As for myself, I always consider myself as one of his Buddhist brothers. So, as a close friend—or as his brother—I always remember him, and I always admire his activities and his lifestyle. Since my meeting with him, and so often when I examine myself, I closely follow some of his examples. Occasionally I really have a deep satisfaction knowing that I have made some contribution regarding his wishes for the world. And so for the rest of my life, the impact of meeting him will remain until my last breath. I really want to state that I make this commitment, and this will remain until my last breath.

service to the world

*A*lso, through my dialogue with Christian monasticism I have found that one of its most impressive aspects is service to society. That, I feel, is one very, very practical contribution to the world. I am concerned that Buddhist monastics make very few practical contributions.

Today, the world has become smaller and smaller and everything is now interdependent. In the past, Buddhist practitioners, particularly monks, have remained distant from society in their own small circle. When that is taken to an extreme, there is negligence or indifference about what is happening in the larger society or in government. There may have been some grounds for such isolation in the past, but today things are changing.

So I think that the Buddhist clergy and monastics should develop a more sensitive conscience about what is really happening in the world. I find this to be important. With such a conscience, eventually a small voice will come from an individual. Then a group of monks—or a Buddhist community—will express its concern and we can change the world for the better.

Frankly speaking, during the last thirty-seven years in exile I think that we Tibetan Buddhists, including myself, have developed closer relationships with our Christian brothers and sisters than with our fellow Buddhists. Although we Tibetans live in India, Thailand, Sri Lanka, Burma, Cambodia, and other Asian countries, we only occasionally visit and greet other Buddhists. On some occasions, we have had some very useful discussions, but these are entirely on an individual basis. Also, our official visits in these countries are difficult due to political and other reasons.

Therefore I think we need to have more contact on a regular basis and bigger meetings—like Buddhist conferences—where ideas can be discussed among ourselves. Then, eventually it will be possible to develop some kind of concrete method for dealing with issues concerning Buddhism and the modern world. My wish is that within our own Buddhist community

—particularly among the monastics and scholars—we should have more international conferences. Such discussion in this current world situation would be very, very helpful.

As for Christianity, because of your large numbers and because you are so materially advanced in the West, I think you can be of great spiritual and material help to building world peace. The other day in England, I jokingly told an audience that once they were the greatest imperialist nation and they exploited people around the world. Now the time has come to pay the world back. So, in terms of the promotion of spiritual and material development, I feel you can do even more.

In parts of Africa and Asia, many people are struggling just to live. Under those circumstances, there is an urgent need for material aid. In responding to these basic human needs, I think that the advanced Western Christian nations have the potential to initiate a new appreciation of the value of human life. Here, I think, our Christian brothers and sisters can make a great contribution.

Also, the most awful weapons, including nuclear weapons, along with the Marxist ideology have come from the West. So in the past, Western nations made some very destructive initiatives in other parts of the world. Now, I think, the time has come to develop more constructive worldwide initiatives. That is my hope and my wish.

Finally let me say that because of the Buddhist–Christian dialogue, we Tibetan Buddhists have developed the best and closest relations with our Christian brothers and sisters. So, dialogue is also one of your great contributions. It builds a healthy spirit of harmony on the basis of mutual understanding. With full knowledge of our differences and our similarities, we have developed mutual respect and mutual understanding. I think this is a good example to other religious traditions and to the world!

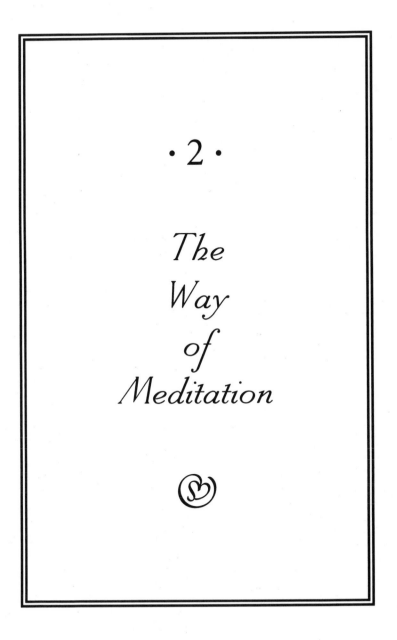

· 2 ·

*The
Way
of
Meditation*

I am now going to speak about the unique Buddhist practice of what is called meditation or contemplation. I will try to explain something which can be useful and may be adopted by Christian practitioners. This can be, I think, a way to enrich one another.

I am not going to talk about whether there is a Creator or not. This is too complicated; and anyway I think it is beyond our concepts. In that regard, it is better to follow one's own belief. Then you can achieve some kind of satisfactory result. Otherwise, the issue is too complicated. For centuries there have been great debates in India between Buddhist logicians and non-Buddhist logicians. The result is that the argument is still going on! So, it is better to follow according to one's own belief. The important thing is to practice, to implement one's belief sincerely and seriously.

So now we will deal with Buddhist approaches to meditation. The Tibetan word for meditation is *sgom*, which appears in scriptures but is actually part and parcel of ordinary daily life. It means familiarizing yourself with certain particular objects or attitudes. Take for example when we feel emotionally afflicted from seeing an object that makes us feel unhappy. We use some kind of *analytical meditation* that includes reasoning. The more we investigate, the more the afflictive emotion develops. And then, after becoming familiar with that object, you will be able to come to a conclusion, or a sort of conviction. You will realize, "Oh, this is something positive!" or "This is something negative!"

This conviction of mind is a form of *single-pointedness meditation*. So, we always use analytical meditation and single-pointedness meditation in our daily life. The very purpose of meditation is to familiarize ourselves with any object or attitude we want to know more about. That is the meaning of meditation as familiarization.

meditation for christians

*T*his practice of meditation becomes important for the transformation of our mind. And this must also be true for the Christian practitioner. Of course Christians are seeking help or blessings from God. But spiritual transformation must also involve our own effort. For example, God's blessing is always present; God's grace is always here. But to the nonbeliever, you see, that blessing may not enter his or her life. Or, it may not enter easily because the level of effort from his or her side is missing. So Christian practitioners also need to practice some kind of personal effort in spirituality. And it is here that meditation is valuable.

How can you develop faith in the proper way through meditation? Using our two types of meditation, first you can practice analytical meditation by thinking about how great God is, how merciful God is. After using this analytical meditation some kind of conviction is reached, "Now, yes, definitely this is the

case!" Then, without further investigation, simply set-
tle your mind in that belief, in that deeper faith. This
is single-pointedness meditation. These two forms of
meditation from the Buddhist tradition must go
together. So you see, faith is not just believing in
words. Rather it combines one's own experience and
the Gospel to develop a firm conviction. That is very
important and even necessary in any religion.

There are also two other types of meditation that
can be helpful. In the first type, you focus on a particular object and then meditate on it. In this case, you
take an object of apprehension to mind. An example
of this first type might be when a Christian is aware of
the greatness of God. In that case you have a separate
object as the focus of your meditation. In the second
type of meditation, you cultivate your mind in the
form of an attitude of meditation. An example of the
second type would be when the Christian meditates to
cultivate faith or love. In that kind of meditation, you
cultivate your own mind in the very nature of faith or
love. In Buddhist practice, when we meditate like this
on the attitudes of compassion or loving kindness, our
mind transforms into that kind of mentality.

meditation for buddhists

*L*et us now take the example of the Buddhist awareness of impermanence. Generally speaking, at the beginning this awareness is not through experience but relies on reasons given in the scriptures or someone else's words. But then, one meditates on it using the kinds of analytical and single-pointedness meditations we discussed for Christians.

After much thought and reflection, impermanence becomes familiar. Then, at a certain stage, you realize these reasons and reach a more full conviction concerning impermanence which you can now prove by these reasons with complete confidence. At this stage of meditation, the awareness of impermanence is much firmer than your previous awareness. Of course, you already thought that all things are impermanent, always momentarily changing. But through reasoning in analytical meditation you develop a firm and full conviction.

Then going further without any more reasoning, there is a spontaneous realization of impermanence.

Whenever you see something, without any effort there is a spontaneous realization or awareness of impermanence. In this uncontrived state of vivid realization and developed experience of impermanence, there is a kind of direct perception in which your mind is merged, as it were, with impermanence. From this point of view there is no dualistic appearance.

There are also many other types of meditation objects in Buddhism. One type is called "an object for purifying afflictive emotions." From a Buddhist point of view, over many recent past lifetimes, one has engaged in particular afflictive emotions resulting in a predominant afflictive emotion in this lifetime, such as desire, hatred, confusion, pride, or discursiveness.

Thus, one meditates on an object that will oppose one's predominant afflictive emotion. For instance, in the case of someone who has a lot of hatred, that individual would concentrate on love. In the case of someone who has a lot of desire, that person would concentrate on ugliness. For someone who has a lot of confusion, that individual would meditate on the way that the cyclic round of suffering arises in the process of dependent arising.* For someone who has pride, that individual would reflect on the five mental and physical aggregates or the other constituents of our existence. Someone who is dominated by discursiveness would meditate on the inhalation and exhalation of the breath. So you see, there are a variety of afflictive emotions. And for each afflictive emotion there are different objects on which to meditate in order to lessen these afflictions.

There are also objects of meditation used in Buddhism for the development of "special insight," and for the development of "calm abiding." The difference between calm abiding and special insight is not deter- mined by the respective objects of these different med- itative states. Rather, the difference is determined by how one is engaging the objects. One can engage objects of meditation in ways that produce insight or in ways that produce inner calm. For Buddhists, there is calm abiding that even observes emptiness, and there is also special insight that is observing the varieties of phenomena. Christians too should discover what objects of meditation there are to help them develop

---

* See page 92 for a clarification of the term *dependent arising.*

insight and calm abiding both in relation to faith in God and with regard to developing love for fellow human beings.

practical advice

*D*iet is important when we engage seriously in the practice of meditation. One should follow a light diet which is also very good for the body.

One's daily routine is also important. Getting up early in the morning is very good. Some people, particularly in the city, do the opposite. They stay up very late and are very busy and fully alert at night. Then they are sleeping peacefully after the sun rises the next morning. For a practitioner, that kind of lifestyle is very bad. So, get up early in the morning—"The freshness of early morning, the freshness of our mind." And for that you need sufficient sleep by going to bed early.

Then there is the question of posture. Generally this is also quite important. You should sit straight. The Buddhist justification for this posture is that if you remain straight then your body energy circulates more normally. If you sit one-sided then the body may not be so balanced. Therefore, you should consider this important. But, I do not think it is very important to sit cross-legged. For some people, instead of helping meditation it causes more pain. So, I do not think it is very important. You can find a more comfortable posture if you wish.

According to Buddhist tradition, sometimes one may get some kind of extraordinary understanding or awareness. Take faith for example. Sometimes, without a particular reason, some kind of spontaneous feeling may occur. But from our tradition such an experience—while very positive—is not so reliable. One day faith may be there spontaneously, but the next day it may not. However, once you get that kind of spontaneous experience of faith, it is very useful if you maintain and sustain that faith through effort. So you should not rely too much on just spontaneous experience. It comes and goes, comes and goes. The other more sustained experience of faith, developed through continuous effort, is much more reliable.

an alert mind

I think that in both analytical meditation and single-pointedness meditation the important thing is one's sharpness of mind, having a fully alert mind. This is very, very important. Now, in analytical meditation, a sharpness of mind is essential for the analytical process. But in single-pointedness meditation, fully alert clarity of the mind must also be maintained. Otherwise, sometimes the experience of single-pointedness develops as a result of darkness. This is not at all helpful. You must remain fixed on the object of meditation with full alertness.

Without alertness, there is the danger of mistaking a mental sinking for one-pointed meditation. You see, as your alertness reduces, so the movement of the mind automatically reduces. At that moment you may get the feeling that your mind is really focusing on the object. And you may also feel some kind of tranquillity. That kind of tranquillity is neither positive nor constructive. If you cultivate this negative kind of tranquillity, the sharpness of your mind will be reduced. This is very harmful. So, it is very, very important to keep a sharp and fully alert mind.

How can you keep full alertness? When your mental energy goes down, then an uplifted state of the mind does not occur. For example, if you start single-pointedness meditation, and your mind at that moment is in a slightly sad mood, then that mood automatically reduces the alertness of mind. So at that time you need to extend some effort in order to heighten the state or spirit of your mind.

One method for a Christian would be to think about God's grace or mercy and to reflect on how fortunate we are. Thinking of these kinds of things, which make you feel happy with more hope and more self-confidence, will uplift your mind.

Sometimes you experience the opposite, namely, your mind may be too excited. That state of mind is also a great hindrance to single-pointedness. When you are about to do single-pointedness meditation and your mind is too distracted due to excitement, then think about the fact that because of this kind of mental attitude your spiritual practice, your spiritual experience, will not develop much. Think that because of this excited state you will experience a failure of single-pointedness of mind. Then, you see, your excitement will become a little reduced. When you see your mind come down a little bit, then with that cooler basis go on to meditate. So, these are methods for avoiding mental dullness and excitement in meditation.

a typical day

Finally, let me add something about meditation during a typical day in my own life. I must say that I am a very poor practitioner. Usually I get up at 3:30 in the morning. Then I immediately do some recitations and some chanting. Following this until breakfast, I do meditation, analytical meditation mainly. Then after each analytical meditation, I do single-pointedness meditation. The object of my meditation is mainly dependent arising. Because of dependent arising, things are empty. This is according to the Madhyamika philosophy of Nagarjuna and the interpretation of Chandrakirti.

So, meditating on this gives me a kind of firm conviction of the possibility of the cessation of afflictive emotions. This is one main object of my practice. Another is compassion. These two are my objects of practice. If you ask me about experience in my practice, I think it is better than zero. On that basis, I can assure you that the mind is always changing, so no matter how strong the afflictive emotion, there is always the possibility of change. Transformation is always possible. So therefore, you see, there is always hope. I think that what is really worthwhile is to make an effort.

Then also, in the Tibetan Buddhist tradition, Buddhist *tantrayana* is also involved. So you see, a lot of time is also spent on visualization in deity yoga.* This includes visualizing the process of death and rebirth. In fact in my daily prayer or practice, I visualize death eight times and rebirth eight times. This is not necessarily the Dalai Lama's reincarnation, but some reincarnation. These practices I feel are very powerful and very helpful in familiarizing oneself about the process of death. So when death actually comes, one is prepared. Whether these practices of preparation are really going to benefit me at the time of death, I do not know at this moment.

---

* See page 97 for a clarification of the term *deity yoga*.

I suppose that even with all this preparation for death, I may still be a complete failure! That is also possible.

There is another type of meditation which is like praying. Its purpose is to recollect the various levels and stages of the path by going through something that you have memorized and reflecting on each stage.

So from around 3:30 A.M. until 8:30 A.M. I am fully occupied with meditation and prayer, and things like that. During that time I take a few breaks, including my breakfast—which is usually at 5:00 A.M.—and some prostrations. After 8:30 A.M., when my mood is good, I do some physical exercise. One very important thing is that I always listen to the BBC for the news. Then I do office work until noon. And if it is a holiday, I also start reading important texts. Prayer and meditation are usually done without any texts. Then at noon, I have my lunch. Afterward usually I go to the office and do some more work. At 6:00 P.M., I have my evening tea and dinner as a Buddhist monk. Finally, around 8:30 P.M., I go to sleep—my most favorite, peaceful meditation!

· 3 ·

The
Path
to
Calm Abiding

*T*here is a state of meditation called "calm abiding." While I will be speaking about it from Buddhist texts, this practice is common to both Buddhists and non-Buddhists. For instance, in India both Buddhists and non-Buddhists have practiced it. Therefore, I feel that our Christian brothers and sisters also could practice this form of meditation.

overcoming obstacles

*W*ith respect to achieving the state of calm abiding, there are five faults, or five factors that oppose its development; and there are eight antidotes to those five faults. The first fault is laziness. With respect to this first fault, laziness, there are four antidotes. These include faith, aspiration, exertion, and pliancy.

Faith here means faith in the qualities of meditative stabilization. Aspiration is the aspiration to attain meditative stabilization and is induced by faith. Exertion means to exert oneself to attain meditative stabilization. As for the last antidote, pliancy, at this point one does not have pliancy, but one can consider its advantages. Among these advantages is that the body, compared to its usual state, will be very light and pliant. Also, you will be able to set your mind in whatever virtue you want. Thus, as an antidote to laziness, you can contemplate the good qualities of pliancy that will be achieved through overcoming laziness.

With regard to the types of laziness, often there is the type in which you feel, "Oh, I am not capable of doing this; I am inferior; I could not possibly do this!" Although this attitude is not often mentioned explicitly, it is very important to counteract this psychological sense of inferiority. This can be done through reflecting on various encouraging tenets. One good way for a Buddhist to do this is to reflect on the Buddha-nature that is within everyone, and is therefore within oneself.

Also, a Buddhist could reflect on the marvelous situation of leisure and fortune that is difficult to attain and that one has already attained. One has a human body with a lifetime that gives one enough time to practice—and the conditions to practice—the spiritual life. Through reflecting on this fact, one can realize what a good situation one is in and thus overcome the laziness of feeling inferior.

From a Christian point of view, one could reflect on the fact that God's grace is always present, that the blessings of God are always there ready to be received. With this point of view, one can overcome the kind of laziness which entails the feeling that "I cannot possibly do this!"

The second fault, namely, the forgetting of the object on which you are meditating, is overcome through mindfulness. The function of mindfulness is to keep from being distracted to other objects. Mindfulness can only work on an object with which you are familiar, with which you have developed an acquaintance. Then, by developing mindfulness, it can serve its function of preventing distraction to other objects. It is mainly through developing the dexterity of mindfulness that one can achieve calm abiding.

mindfulness

To develop strong mindfulness, it is important to act mindfully in all aspects of your behavior. Whether you are walking about or standing, whether you are sitting down or even lying down, it is important to maintain mindfulness of what you are doing.

In order to maintain mindfulness continuously, it is necessary to have conscientiousness. This is very important for all religious practitioners. And this is why it is necessary to have an ethical foundation in the development of calm abiding. That is, ethical behavior requires that one maintain mindfulness of what one is doing, and conscientiousness with respect to what one is doing. That mindfulness and conscientiousness developed in moral practice will also help in one's meditation.

Silence is also very, very important to the practice of mindfulness. The reason for this is that we have many different thoughts, many different ideas, that run through our minds. Those thoughts arise as if following after sounds. Language itself, therefore, induces a lot of different thoughts. But when one remains silent, in time this silence will gradually reduce the number of thoughts. In Dharamsala, there is a fellow religious practitioner who from time to time spends a month in total silence. But on Saturdays, he will talk. Sometimes this person will engage in this practice for several months. Through supports such as these, the object of meditation is held by the power of mindfulness.

scattering

The third fault is laxity and excitement. Its antidote is introspection. If one has developed powerful mindfulness, introspection will come of itself. But the special way to develop introspection is from time to time to inspect what is happening with your body and your mind. With regard to laxity, its coarser form is like darkness in which the subject loses the object. In the subtler form of laxity, the object is clear enough but there is a lack of clarity within the subject. That is, the consciousness that is paying attention to the object is itself unclear. In this case, there is a great danger in confusing this subtle laxity with real meditation.

It is also true that "scattering"—that is, distraction—to any type of object is a serious fault to developing meditation. However, desire is singled out as an important cause of scattering because everyone has a great deal of distraction due to objects of desire. Thus, excitement, meaning here desirous excitement, is emphasized and is often mentioned in place of scattering.

Any type of scattering is harmful. For instance, if you are meditatively cultivating faith in God, and during that period you scatter to another object such as the cultivation of compassion, then that distraction is something that needs to be stopped at that time. Even though the meditative cultivation of compassion is something that in general you should do, it should be done at another time. The same is true with regard to meditatively cultivating compassion. If at that time you scatter to developing faith in God, then that faith-developing meditation needs to be stopped at that time.

As an illustration, what one is trying to do here is like starting a fire and keeping it going by adding fuel to it. If rather than adding fuel you do something else—even something good—you are letting the fire diminish or die down, and you are going to have to begin all over again. Similarly, when laxity and excitement arise, one's mind easily comes under their power.

balance

*I*t is also a fault not to apply the antidotes to laxity and excitement. This would be an example of the fourth fault, namely, the "nonapplication of antidotes." Furthermore, the antidotes to laxity are all within the class of raising the mode of apprehension of the mind. The antidotes to excitement are within the class of allowing the mode of apprehension of the mind to diminish a little bit.

When you have applied the antidotes to laxity or excitement, and whichever one of them is bothering you does in fact diminish, if you keep applying that antidote then that activity itself turns into a fault. This is the fifth and final fault, the "over-application of the antidotes." In this case, you simply have to stop applying the antidote.

calm abiding

*L*et us now look at the experience that one goes through on the path to calm abiding. First is the stage called "setting the mind," where one is trying to set the mind on the object of meditation. When through effort one is able to keep the mind set more continuously on the object, this stage is called "continuous setting." Then, through noticing scattering and putting the mind back on the object, one attains the point where two-thirds of the time one is able to stay concentrated on the object. This stage is called "resetting." When one is more effective with regard to applying the antidotes to coarse laxity and excitement, one attains the fourth stage which is called "close setting." Then, as one deals with subtle laxity and excitement and overcomes them, one passes through the fifth stage (called "disciplining"), the sixth stage (called "pacifying"), the seventh stage (called "thorough pacifying"), the eighth stage (called "making one-pointed"), and finally the ninth stage (called "setting in equipoise").

As it is stated in the Buddhist texts, when one reaches this ninth stage, one has reached a level of single-pointedness meditation which is still included within the "desire realm." In Buddhism, we speak of there being three realms: the desire realm, the form realm, and the formless realm. Setting in equipoise is categorized within the desire realm.

While this ninth stage itself is not calm abiding, through continuous meditation at this stage one develops calm abiding. Both Buddhist and Hindu sources present this calm abiding as the initial preparation for a level of meditation called the "first concentration." Thus, calm abiding is called the "not unable" because through its cultivation one is able to achieve the first concentration. Then through further continuous cultivation, one can achieve the second, third, and fourth concentrations. These four concentrations are included within the form realm. Besides these four concentrations, there are also the four higher states called absorptions that are included within the formless realm. The objects of these absorptions include limitless space, limitless consciousness, so-called nothingness, and the peak of cyclic existence.

For our Christian brothers and sisters, I think that the four concentrations and the four formless absorptions are not needed. What you need is the development of calm abiding, or the level of one-pointedness of mind that is included within the so-called desire realm. The purpose of developing this calm abiding is so that you can have very firm, positive qualities of mind, such as faith. The stability of this kind of meditation will make your faith very strong. The actual content of faith, and other spiritual qualities of mind, can then be understood and described according to one's respective religious tradition.

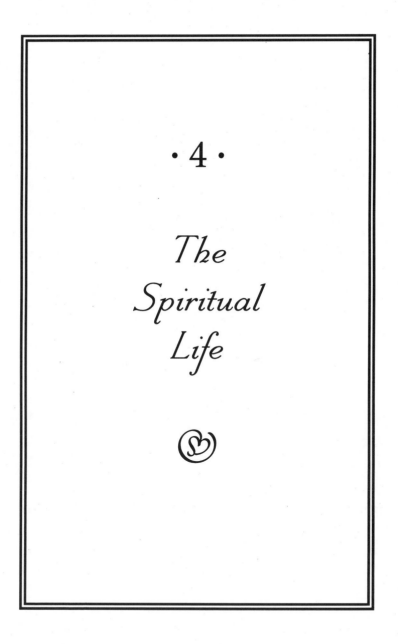

· 4 ·

The
Spiritual
Life

*F*or somebody who has an interest in the spiritual life—which for us is embodied in the *bodhisattva*'s* attitude, deeds, and activities—it is important to understand that it is necessary to have concern for the welfare of society and a strong relationship with society.

charity

*I*n a *bodhisattva*'s practice, there are the six perfections, among which the first is the perfection of giving, of charity. Within giving there are three types: (1) giving

---

* A *bodhisattva* is a person who undertakes the path to Buddhahood for the benefit of all living beings.

material things; (2) giving the *Dharma*, or the religious teaching; and (3) giving "non-fright," that is, relieving beings of fear. All three types of charity, the giving of material things, the giving of teaching, and the giving of non-fright, are necessarily connected with society. Our Christian brothers and sisters are also implementing these forms of giving in the fields of social service, education, and health care.

In order to serve effectively in the community, you have to live in society. Because of this, there is a danger that this social involvement may weaken your own spiritual practice. Therefore, during the initial period of the spiritual life, the important thing is to develop strong mental qualities according to the *bodhisattva* teaching. Once you gain the necessary inner strength and self-confidence that can maintain your spiritual life under difficult circumstances, that is the right time to involve yourself in society.

While in society carrying out charity or service in daily life, you should also spend time on your own spiritual practice. This is just like recharging a battery. Then, you can use that charge as power for the rest of the day. I think this is very important. Our Christian brothers and sisters should follow this same pattern. Although you may be involved fully in the field of education or the field of social welfare, there is no point in neglecting your own spiritual practice. Social activities and spiritual practice go side by side.

morality and patience

*A*mong the six perfections of the *bodhisattva* life, the second is the practice of ethics. The main idea in the practice of ethics for *bodhisattvas* is to restrain concern only for oneself and to live more fully for the benefit of others. Then the third perfection is the practice of forbearance or patience. There are three types of patience: (1) not being concerned about any harm that might come to oneself, (2) voluntarily accepting hardships, and (3) the patience or forbearance involved in ascertaining the doctrine.

With regard to a selfless ethics that benefits others, and also in regard to patiently accepting hardships and lacking self-concern, Buddhists find a complete similarity here with the practice of our Christian brothers and sisters. Especially their monastic way of life deliberately fosters morality, simplicity, and contentment. Even their food is simple. In fact, after an exchange program, one group of our monks returned from their tour in the United States. I met with them and they expressed how much they enjoyed visiting Christian monasteries. They gained a lot of experiences, and—most importantly—their attitude toward Christianity was also very much changed. Their only complaint was that in some monasteries they remained half-hungry after meals. Through the kindness of some of their new friends, they were able to get some more biscuits.

I also think that the genuine Christian practice of poverty, even in meals, is very valuable for reducing greed or attachment. And there is no doubt that Christian monastics practice patience and tolerance. If somebody hits them on one cheek, they turn the other. That is the Gospel, and it is clearly the same practice as ours.

In Buddhism, there is also forbearance with respect to ascertaining the meaning of the doctrine. Here too, the basic pattern is the same for both our traditions. For the Buddhist, in considering very difficult subjects such as emptiness, at the initial stage you might find it difficult to accept or understand. In that case, you need patience. Similarly with regard to Christian belief or faith in God, sometimes you may experience doubt. In that case, you need this forbearance with respect to ascertaining the meaning of having faith in God.

effort

Now we come to the fourth *bodhisattva* perfection, which is effort. Every religious practitioner needs effort. By effort we mean an enthusiasm for the practice of virtue. On the positive side, this means to pay attention to what needs to be achieved. On the negative side, it means to overcome the forces opposing such effort, that is, the various types of laziness. One type of laziness is attachment to the meaningless activities of worldly life. Another is the laziness of thinking, "I could not possibly do this!" This is really a matter of having low self-esteem. The other form of laziness is procrastination.

Since these are problems faced by all religious practitioners, the practices of effort are also for everyone.

wisdom

The fifth perfection is of concentration, about which we have already spoken, so let us go on to the sixth perfection, namely, the perfection of wisdom. Here I will try to explain the Buddhist notion of wisdom and its ultimate type, namely, the realization of emptiness.

Among the types of wisdom, there is the wisdom knowing the varieties of phenomena, and the wisdom knowing the mode of being of phenomena. Between these two, the latter—the wisdom knowing the mode of being or the ultimate nature of phenomena—is more important. This wisdom is the wisdom realizing emptiness.

What should be understood by the word *emptiness*? There are many different ways of positing the meaning of emptiness. On one level, it means understanding that the person is not permanent, unitary, and self-powered. Within Buddhism, all schools agree on this type of understanding of emptiness. Then, a subtler level is the emptiness of the self-sufficiency of the person. By self-sufficient personhood we mean that the person has a nature, and that the mind and body have natures other than the nature of the person. This is like a lord and two subjects; that is, the lord (person) is distinct in nature from the subjects (mind and body). Emptiness means that there is no personhood (lord) separate from the mind and body (subjects)—that there is an emptiness of this type of personhood. Then there is another related level of misconception of the nature of the person in which one sees the person and the mind and body as of the same essential nature, but still conceives of the person as being like the boss and the mind and body as being like subjects that are bossed around.

In the Mind-Only School and the Middle Way School of Buddhism, they also speak about a misconception of a "self-of-phenomena" and an emptiness of a "self-of-phenomena." The Mind-Only School speaks of two types of basic misconceptions in this regard. One is the misconception that subject and object are different entities. The other is the misconception that phenomena exist by way of their own character as referents of our words and our conceptual thoughts about them. Thus, the Mind-Only School teaches that there is an emptiness of these two types of status.

In the Middle Way School, they speak about the misconception that phenomena truly or ultimately exist. Since that is taken as what is to be negated, they also speak of an emptiness of the true or ultimate existence of phenomena. Within the Middle Way School, further distinctions are made. One tradition, the Autonomy School, holds that the phenomena that appear to a nondefective consciousness—a consciousness that does not have any superficial types of errors—do indeed truly exist conventionally. Thus, what do they posit as true existence when they say that phenomena are empty of true existence? For this tradition, the false status is that phenomena are not posited through the force of appearing to a nondefective consciousness, but are established by way of their own unique mode of being. This status is the true existence that is being negated or declared empty.

Then in the other Middle Way School, called the Consequence School, the final thought of Nagarjuna is described by Buddhapalita, Chandrakirti, and Shantideva.

In this final system, the way phenomena appear to non-defective consciousness—as if they exist in their own right—is itself taken as what is to be negated in emptiness. Phenomena actually do not exist in that way; they exist only nominally. Thus, emptiness is the absence of this exaggerated status of phenomena—as if they exist from their own side. So, the emptiness of such inherent existence of phenomena is the subtlest selflessness of phenomena. Finally, it is this fact that is realized by wisdom.

love and compassion

*B*esides the six perfections in the Buddhist spiritual life, I want to mention something in the Buddhist texts that I think is also very appropriate for our Christian sisters and brothers. This is the importance of cultivating an altruistic intention to develop oneself spiritually for the sake of others.

In this cultivation process, first one realizes that one has self-cherishing and lacks the cherishing of others.

Then we should reflect on the disadvantages of cherishing oneself and the advantages of cherishing others. Through this process of meditation, self-cherishing is diminished and the cherishing of others is developed. In this case, you develop what is called a neglecting of yourself and an emphasis on the welfare of others.

This does not mean that you should neglect your own situation entirely. In order even to develop a sense of cherishing others, you have to know what it means to cherish yourself. Selflessness does not mean just to forget oneself. Rather, what one must reduce is any selfish feeling which leads one to exploit the other or to harm the other. Generally, low self-esteem is very negative. I think that low self-esteem, or hating yourself, is really sad. It is not good at all.

When we deal with different mental emotions, we have to know precisely what is positive and what is negative. For example, there are two kinds of desire. The desire to have more happiness or the desire to be close to God, these kinds of desires are very constructive. Other desires, like wanting all sorts of things, eventually lead us to disappointment and disaster. Also, there can be two kinds of anger. One form of anger, which is motivated by compassion, is in a real sense very constructive. But anger which eventually develops into hatred, that kind of anger is absolutely negative. So we have to make distinctions.

The ego feeling, the sense of a strong self, is also of two kinds. One is the feeling that "I can work hard in order to serve others! I must dedicate myself for the welfare of others!" In order to develop such a willful determination, we need a strong sense of self that is very positive. The other kind of ego feeling leads to harming another with no hesitation. That kind of strong ego feeling is very negative. Again, we have to make distinctions when we deal with different emotions in developing love and compassion.

I would like to suggest that to cultivate compassion in the spiritual life one can take as an object of meditation sentient beings who are full of suffering and then wish that they become free from suffering. To cultivate love, one can take as one's object of meditation beings who are bereft of happiness and then develop the wish that they become endowed with happiness.

In both the case of compassion and of love, you should be unbiased. Usually, because of our feelings toward our own close friends, we may have some kind of natural concern about their welfare. That is not necessarily true compassion because it is mixed with attachment. So, that is a biased feeling that is directed only toward a limited number of persons. Also, because our friends' attitude toward us is positive, as a response we feel a close feeling. This is not genuine love.

Genuine compassion and love do not regard what kind of attitude the other has toward you. Rather, on the basis of realizing that others are just like oneself—they too want happiness, they too do not want suffering, and they also have the right to overcome suffering—on that basis, one can develop a true sense of concern. There is genuine love and compassion which is not biased and even extends toward one's enemy.

Now, how can you develop that kind of concern? The way to develop love and compassion is first of all to visualize a being whose level of suffering is such that, to our ordinary mind, we feel we cannot bear it. We just do not even want to look at it. Take that person to mind and reflect on the qualities of his or her suffering. Then reflect on the fact that he or she is similar to yourself in terms of wanting happiness and not wanting suffering.

Through time, you will very strongly feel a sense of concern for that other person. That is how love and compassion are developed.

Then move your meditation to other persons who are close to you one by one. Eventually work on your enemies, one by one, taking them to mind and seeing that they are similar to yourself in wanting happiness, not wanting suffering, and having the right to be free from suffering. Thus, you can develop the same strength of concern with respect to them. It is important that we emphasize developing love and compassion with respect to those beings who are hard to care for. In the Gospels, there is also the same message about the need to develop patience and forbearance in loving one's enemies. Here is the real basis of the spiritual life in which we live for the sake of others, for the sake of benefiting the world.

· 5 ·

The

Spiritual

Guide

Not only does the *bodhisattva* affect society in his or her compassionate practice of the six perfections, but also as a teacher and role model of this spiritual way of life and its wisdom. According to the *bodhisattva* vehicle, a *bodhisattva's* practices are twofold. First, one must perform the practice of the six perfections in order to ripen or mature his or her mental continuum. Then, with respect to teaching others, that person should also have what are called the "four means of gathering students." First is to give material things to students. Second is to speak pleasantly—giving greetings and showing concern. Third is to teach students what is to be adopted in practice and what is to be gotten rid of in their behavior. Fourth is to practice oneself what one teaches to others. When a guru teaches a student how to behave and does not practice what he or she teaches, then the student will say, "Well, you should be doing it first! You should practice this yourself!"

teachings

There are two types of Buddhist teaching: scriptural teaching and realizational teaching. These teachings are approached by way of explanation and by way of practice. And it is in connection with these approaches to teaching that the spiritual community is important.

In Christianity, the spiritual community is also very important. In Buddhism, it is on the basis of the full functioning of a certain number of monastics that you can determine whether the Buddha's teaching is a living practice or not. When the monastic community observes the three basic monastic practices, then we can say that the Buddha's teaching is still alive. So too the teachings of Christ should be lived by the Christian community.

After Buddha was enlightened, he began to teach the rules of discipline to guide people in following the

Buddhist way. Eventually, Buddha taught the *Pratimoksha,* which is our lineage of monastic precepts. It is said that Buddhas are teachers of refuge, and that the *Dharma*—the realized scriptural teaching—is the actual refuge. The sisters and brothers helping people to this refuge are the *Sangha* community. It is said that the *Sangha* is like nurses and attendants taking care of sick persons. Thus, the community is a group that indeed has to work and proceed together in realizing the *Dharma* in the world. Without a community that has internalized the practices, the discipline, and so forth, there is no Buddhist teaching. Buddha said that when there is a *Sangha,* a spiritual community that has internalized these practices, then he can feel very relaxed.

celibacy

*I*n terms of our precepts, I would like to say something about celibacy. This is a common practice for both Buddhist and Christian monks and nuns. However, we have different ideas concerning the practice of celibacy. In Buddhism, our goal is *moksha* (liberation) or

Nirvana. What is Nirvana? It is the complete elimination of afflictive emotions. Among the afflictive emotions, according to all Buddhist schools of thought, desire, or attachment, is one of the key factors which bind a person in the cyclic existence of suffering. In this regard, sexual desire is one of the more serious sorts of attachment. And since our goal is to overcome these attachments, the practice of celibacy becomes important. This is the Buddhist understanding of the practice of celibacy.

The Christian concept of celibacy may be different, but the result is the same. Both say that the monastic— or priest in the Christian tradition—should not engage in sexual practice. The reasons do not matter; what is important is that the practice of celibacy in both tradi- tions is similar.

Now concerning this practice, sometimes it may appear as if it were against human nature. This is because sexuality is a natural biological force and criti- cal for human reproduction. Therefore, celibacy is not easy. But at the same time it is spiritually very important. So, in practicing celibacy we need a firm determination on the basis of an awareness of the disadvantage of sex- ual practice and the advantage of celibacy.

I think that in order to gain this awareness it is useful to examine the layperson's lifestyle. For example, look at those couples who have no children and worry a great deal about having a child. Or perhaps they begin to have children; then they may worry about having too many children. So, then they worry about birth control. That too is very difficult: birth control, and worst is abortion. This also brings mental troubles, mental burdens. And once you have a family, half of your freedom is already lost. So, maybe people with families or those who have love experiences have a life that is very colorful. But I think that this kind of life has too many burdens.

So while our life may be less colorful, our mental stability is much more steady. And in the long run, that is also good for one's health. I think it is very useful to think of the value of celibacy along these lines. Even in the short run there are advantages—such as mental stability—to a lifestyle with celibacy. In the long run, celibacy is a great help in the Buddhist way to achieve freedom from cyclic existence. And in the Christian way, celibacy also is helpful to the development of greater devotion to God and other aspects of the spiritual life as well as service to others.

rules

*I*n Buddhism there are general rules that are for all monks and nuns, and there are also rules that are specific to particular monasteries. The same is true in Christianity where there are general rules that all monks and nuns keep, and there are also particular rules that are kept by certain monastics. For example, I have noticed that in some monasteries, after finishing the meal at lunchtime, each monk washes his own spoons and forks. This for me is a new experience!

It is very, very important to have strict rules in monastic life. This is not a matter of imposing rules by force. Rather, one first examines himself or herself to see if, because of certain reasons, there is an attraction to becoming a monk or nun. Then when one makes up his or her mind, he or she voluntarily takes on this discipline.

Rules are very important aids in pursuing the spiritual life in all religious traditions. Since some aids are more essential in cultivating the spiritual life than others, in our type of discipline generally there are practices that must be kept tightly, and others that can be kept more loosely. Some people are more strict than others. I prefer to be more strict. I think strictness is very beneficial because when one becomes lax in the spiritual life, then it is something like a small crack and the laxity eventually becomes greater and greater. So, it is very important to be more strict right from the beginning.

the spiritual teacher

Now something else about the spiritual teacher that may be helpful to Christians as well as to Buddhists. For there to be a good and strong spiritual community, there must be teachers who teach the path well; and for that, they must provide proper role models. Teaching about spiritual matters does not just take place on the intellectual level. The teacher must also show what is taught to his or her followers by example. The teacher must provide an example for the eyes of his or her followers. Then the students will develop a genuine appreciation and respect. If the teacher says one thing and does something else, how can the students develop genuine respect? And without that respect, how can the teacher guide the students in the spiritual life? True spiritual guidance is not done by force, but arises from respect and devotion freely given. So to have a teacher of the highest quality—such as Thomas Merton—is extremely important.

In the Buddhist texts, they speak of three different qualities that the teacher must have: the teacher (1) must be learned, (2) must be disciplined, and (3) must have a good heart. As was said in an earlier Tibetan tradition, one must have learnedness that does not hinder the discipline, and one must have discipline that does not prevent learnedness. One needs to have a union of both learnedness and discipline. But, even though one has both learnedness and discipline, if one does not have a good heart then one cannot sufficiently help others.

a spiritual relationship

The relationship between the teacher and student is also very important. Since the relationship between the student and the teacher is developed within a religious context, it has an impact on the implementation of the student's religious practice. Teachers in a sense are not appointed. It is the student who chooses a teacher, who makes that person into his or her guru, because the teacher has certain spiritual qualities.

Therefore at the beginning, the student's side of the relationship is absolutely crucial. It is necessary for the student to watch, to check, to investigate whether a person has the proper qualities to be a guru—whether that person is really reliable or not. At the beginning in particular this kind of examination or investigation is extremely important. Otherwise, if you just hurriedly accept a person as your guru without much investigation, as time goes on you may find some fault in that person. Then, you could lose respect for your teacher and that is not good for a spiritual practitioner.

Because the qualities of a good teacher in the student–teacher relationship are of such great importance, Buddha himself spoke very clearly about the different types of qualifications that various levels of teachers must have. For example, Buddha spoke in great detail about the qualifications for a teacher of laypersons, of those receiving novice ordination, and of those receiving full ordination. At all these levels in the community, the true guru—with learnedness, discipline, and a good heart—guides practitioners with instruction and by personal example.

my personal gurus

I personally have had seventeen gurus from different Buddhist lineages. There were two official tutors from whom I received teaching for the longest period of time. One gave me *bhiksu* ordination when I was about six or seven. Then he took full responsibility for my education. I remember that when I was small, he very rarely smiled. I was really very much afraid of him, and on a few occasions he scolded me. That, of course, is the Tibetan tradition.

Sometimes the teacher even uses a whip. For the young Dalai Lama there is a particular whip. When I started my study my immediate elder brother was also with me. So, my teacher prepared two whips—one for me and one for him. The only difference was that my whip was yellow. Except for the color the whips were the same, so the pain was the same. The color did not make any difference! My teacher always kept that whip beside him; but, fortunately, he never used it on me. However, on a few occasions he threatened to use it. My poor elder brother did receive the blessing of the whip on a few occasions.

Now I realize that when I was a very young student I did not think properly. So my tutor's sternness was suitable. A story will show why. When I was small, one lama from the search party was—at the initial stage—an acting tutor. Since he was very jovial and very peaceful, we became very close friends. When he came to give me my lesson, instead of reading or reciting, I would ride on his back and tell him, "You should chant! You should read!" I was that kind of student.

As Aryadeva says in his *Four-Hundred Stanzas on the Bodhisattva Deeds*, a teacher should interact with students so as to determine first of all their predominant afflictive emotion. Whether this be pride, belligerence, lust, or confusion, the teacher should respond correspondingly. Therefore, he or she should treat some people very softly and other people more strongly, scolding some, for instance, and praising others a lot. The teacher should respond accordingly and always out of a motivation of altruism.

So, I think my tutor's sternness was very appropriate. Also, he always had a caring attitude. And gradually as I grew up, my tutor's attitude toward me softened. He never made any negative comments, and he fully trusted me—always smiling and laughing. It has now been more than ten years since he passed away. Still, very often in my dreams he comes and gives me inspiration. He was a great teacher and a top scholar. At the same time, he never showed off his knowledge. He always remained very humble. If you asked him something, he would say "I don't know. I don't know." If you insisted, he would explain his knowledge with experience. It was something marvelous!

· 6 ·

The
Attainment
of the
Goal

*H*aving discussed the role of the guide in the attainment of liberation, I would like to say something about what it is that makes the realization of Nirvana possible according to Buddhism. There are two factors that make liberation possible: one is that the nature of the mind is clear light and the other is that the defilements of the mind are adventitious, superficial.

the mind of clear light

*W*ith respect to the fact that the nature of the mind is clear light, we can say that the basic nature of the mind is that it has the capacity to know objects. Therefore, since the mind itself has a nature of comprehending objects, ignorance of objects is not due to the nature of the mind but is due to some other obstructive factor. For instance, if you put your hand over your eyes, you will not see anything. That absence of sight is not due to the fact that the eye does not have a nature of seeing or capacity to see. The eye does have a nature of seeing, but something is obstructing its sight.

So then, what are these obstructing factors? In the scriptural collections of the *bodhisattvas*, there are descriptions of two types of obstructions: (1) those factors that are afflictive emotions and prevent liberation from cyclic existence, and (2) those factors that prevent omniscient knowledge.

ignorance

*A*mong the Buddhist systems there are many ways of identifying these two types of obstructions. I am going to give one description based on a text by Nagarjuna. As it is said in Nagarjuna's *Seventy Stanzas on Emptiness*, that which views what arises from causes and conditions as existing as its own reality is ignorance. And from this ignorance, the twelve links of dependent arising, of a lifetime in cyclic existence, arise. Thus, Nagarjuna is saying that a consciousness that views what arises from causes and conditions as being produced in its own right, as existing from its own side, is ignorance.

So then, what is ignorance? Ignorance is a type of consciousness that does not know the actual mode of being of objects, and instead conceives the very opposite of the actual mode of being of objects. As Aryadeva says in his *Four-Hundred Stanzas on the Bodhisattva Deeds*: "The seed of cyclic existence is consciousness, and objects are its sphere of activity; so when selflessness is seen in objects, the seed of cyclic existence ceases."

The first part of the passage literally says, "The seed of cyclic existence is consciousness." If by "consciousness" Aryadeva meant that consciousness in general—or consciousness as such—is the seed of cyclic existence, there would be no way of overcoming cyclic existence. This is because consciousness itself has the nature of luminosity and knowing, and there is nothing that can act as a counteragent to consciousness having such a nature of luminosity and knowing. Thus, Aryadeva's intention here is to refer to a specific type of afflictive consciousness as the seed of cyclic existence.

This becomes clear when Aryadeva says that since objects are the sphere of the activity of consciousness, if one sees selflessness in objects, the process of cyclic existence will cease. What then is this selflessness of objects? As Nagarjuna says in his *Treatise on the Middle*: "Those which are dependent arisings are said to be empty." That which arises by depending on other factors arises relative to something else. That it arises dependently, or relative to something else, is a sign that the object does not exist under its own power. So what does this tell us about ignorance? Ignorance is a consciousness that views what is not inherently existent, or existent under its own power, as existing inherently or under its own power.

In sum, when external and internal objects appear to us, they do not appear to be relative. Rather, they appear to exist in their own right or from their own side. That objects exist in their own right is not factual but is susceptible to refutation by reasoning, and it is not suitable to assert what is contradicted by reasoning. Thus, when objects appear to exist in their own right, in fact they do not so exist.

Through reasoning one can realize that objects do not exist in and of themselves. One can develop greater and greater familiarity with this realization, and overcome the conception of nonrelative existence since these two modes of apprehension are contradictory. Hence, it is said that ignorance has an antidote. Because there is an antidote to ignorance, ignorance is removable. This is why ignorance is called adventitious, superficial. It is by way of these two factors that it is shown that liberation is possible, that liberation is attainable: (1) the mind has a nature of clear light, and (2) defilements of the mind are superficial.

This philosophy is very profound, and, for me, it is really something marvelous. It gives me a kind of conviction about reality—about emptiness—and through that conviction I get the feeling that there is the possibility of eliminating all afflictive emotions. As Nagarjuna says in his *Treatise on the Middle*, by extinguishing contaminated karma and afflictive emotions through wisdom there is liberation. Therefore, liberation is a state of having extinguished contaminated actions and afflictive emotions.

So then, what produces contaminated karma or contaminated actions? Contaminated actions come from afflictive emotions. Then what produces afflictive emotions? They come from improper mental conceptuality, improper mental application. From what, in turn, has such improper mental application arisen? It is produced from conceptual elaborations, that is, elaborations of the mind as it conceives objects to exist truly in their own right. These elaborations are ceased—finally —through meditating on emptiness.

nirvana

What then is Nirvana? Different Buddhist schools of thought have different interpretations of Nirvana. According to Nagarjuna and particularly Chandrakirti, Nirvana is something like a quality of mind. But then, what is that quality? It is not a quality of realization. It is a quality of having separated from defilement. It is the state of having separated from defilements through the application of the antidotes to those defilements. And then, when you look to see what that is, you find the final nature of the mind itself.

The final nature of the mind exists as long as there is the mind, namely, from beginningless time. So, this final nature of the mind is with us from the very start. But only when it becomes endowed with the quality of having separated from defilements through the power of their antidotes is that final nature of the mind called Nirvana. The very basis, the foundation of Nirvana is always with us. It is not something that is sought from the outside. Therefore, some Zen practitioners say that Buddhahood is not to be found outside; it is already inside.

A further distinction is found in the statement that cyclic existence (*samsara*) and Nirvana are the same. This means that the final nature of all phenomena, not just the mind, is the same. When we view phenomena, we see that they are many and various, good and bad. But when we of view their final nature itself, we find that the final nature of all of them is of the same "taste." Thus, it is said that the one taste is diverse, and the diverse has one taste.

From this point of view, cyclic existence should not be looked at as bad and Nirvana as good. Rather, the nature of cyclic existence and the final nature of Nirvana is the same. This position is stated in the sutras and in the tantras. It is also particularly stressed in the Great Completeness System of the Tibetan Nyingma School.

god and deity yoga

We have been speaking about the goal of Nirvana in Buddhism. However, freedom from afflictive emotions is of value to all religious persons, and hopefully our analysis can be helpful to Christians too. Of course for Christians the goal of the spiritual life also involves union with God. This is something different from Nirvana as I have explained it. But, I would like to add that when I speak of God in the sense of "infinite love," Buddhists also can accept that kind of interpretation of God.

There is also another common point between our traditions: Buddhists do accept higher beings. We consider Buddhas, *bodhisattvas*, and *arahants* as higher beings. The difference between them and God is that those higher beings were not in their higher status right from the beginning. They became higher beings by pursuing the spiritual life. Compared with us, they are considered higher beings.

To some extent, we can appeal to these higher beings through prayer. Also, we can obtain certain influences as blessings from these higher beings. But, in the end we place a greater emphasis on our own spiritual effort. According to Buddhist traditions, even these higher beings also gained their position through their own practice. So, we place our main emphasis on our own effort and practice.

With this emphasis in mind, let me say something about deity yoga. The main purpose of deity yoga is not worship, or seeking blessings, or anything like that. The main purpose is to create a union of motivational method and wisdom. How is this to be done? It is achieved by taking the wisdom realizing emptiness itself and using it to appear as an ideal being, that is to say, as a deity. Then, the main purpose of the highest tantric yoga is to minimize the grosser level of consciousness, and to manifest the innermost subtle mind. Once that subtle mind becomes active, it can be transformed into wisdom which understands emptiness.

This transformation of the subtle mind is important because of the following reason. A coarser level of consciousness that realizes emptiness—the emptiness of the inherent existence of phenomena—can act as an antidote to defilements. But if one is able to utilize this subtler level of consciousness and turn it into a wisdom consciousness that realizes emptiness, then since that subtle level of consciousness is more powerful it has a far greater effect in removing these obstructions. And it is by this removal that one progresses in the attainment of Nirvana.

a goal for all

Finally, I would like to point out that the purpose of religion is not to build beautiful churches or temples; it is to cultivate positive human qualities such as tolerance, generosity, and love. Fundamental to Buddhism and Christianity, indeed to every major world religion, is the belief that we must reduce our selfishness and serve others.

Every religion and culture has its distinguishing characteristics. For Tibetans, the emphasis for many centuries has been on developing and upholding inner values such as compassion and wisdom. These are more important to us than acquiring material wealth, fame, or success. We regard inner strength, gentleness, love, compassion, wisdom, and a stable mind as the most important treasures a human being can collect in his or her lifetime.

However, I am aware that this inner search can lead to a kind of peaceful complacency. I feel that we Buddhists have much to learn from our Christian brothers and sisters. We are all aware of the inner peace that can be found in prayer and meditation, but our Christian friends may have a richer experience of bringing that inner peace to bear in practical ways in the generous service of others.

I believe it is extremely important that we extend our understanding of each other's spiritual practices and traditions. This is not necessarily done in order to adopt them ourselves, but to increase our opportunities for mutual respect. Sometimes, too, we encounter something in another tradition that helps us better appreciate

something in our own. All faiths, despite their contradictory philosophies, possess the ability to produce fine
warmhearted human beings. Therefore, there is every
reason to appreciate and respect all forms of spiritual
practice that make better human beings and help create
a happier, more peaceful world.

THOMAS KEATING

OPEN MIND,
OPEN HEART

Written by an acknowledged modern spiritual master, the book moves beyond "discursive meditation and particular acts to the intuitive level of contemplation." Keating gives an overview of the history of contemplative prayer in the Christian tradition, and step-by-step guidance in the method of centering prayer.

158 pages

THOMAS KEATING

THE MYSTERY OF CHRIST
The Liturgy as Christian Experience

A reflection on the contemplative dimension of Christian worship. Focusing on the liturgical year, Abbot Keating shares his theological and mystical perspective on the major feasts of the annual cycle.

160 pages

THOMAS KEATING

INVITATION TO LOVE
The Way of Christian Contemplation

In this final volume of his trilogy, Abbot Keating offers a road map, as it were, for a journey that begins when centering prayer is seriously undertaken.

160 pages

Thomas Keating
CRISIS OF FAITH,
CRISIS OF LOVE
Revised and Expanded Edition

"Under the influence of Christian mystics such as St. John of the Cross, Keating weaves a narrative account of spiritual development that will be of . . . interest to spiritual directors and seekers."　　　　　　　　　*—Booklist*

140 pages

William A. Meninger
THE LOVING
SEARCH FOR GOD
Contemplative Prayer and
The Cloud of Unknowing

"Using the fourteenth-century spiritual classic *The Cloud of Unknowing* as both a jumping-off place and a sustained point of reference, Meninger, a Trappist monk and retreat master, does a powerful job of explaining contemplative prayer and making it approachable for any seeker. In a nurturing, practical, and easy-to-understand manner, and with an obvious affection for his subject, Meninger deals with the yearning search for God through prayer and with the distractions that can impede it—unforgiveness and unforgivenness, will, distortions of imagination, memory, and intellect. The result, filled with humor and built by means of good, solid language that flows beautifully, is an excellent guide for anyone interested in deepening his or her Christian prayer life."

—Publishers Weekly

120 pages

WILLIAM A. MENINGER
THE PROCESS OF FORGIVENESS

In this book, Father Meninger explores the complex, but most necessary facet of spiritual life: forgiveness. He shows how we can learn to make this the most simple, yet most difficult part of our spiritual practice.

112 pages

WILLIAM A. MENINGER
THE TEMPLE OF THE LORD
And Other Stories

Composed in the form of three stories which form a triptych illustrating the spiritual life, the book examines three important facets of Christian understanding: "The Temple of the Lord," "Wisdom Built a House," and "The Messiah God."

96 pages

JOHN R. AURELIO
RETURNINGS
Life-after-Death Experiences: A Christian View

"Easy to read and full of practical insight."

—*Booklist*

"So, very good! What a strength and consolation this will be for many people!" —Richard Rohr

120 pages

M. Basil Pennington
ON RETREAT WITH THOMAS MERTON

Fellow Cistercian monk and intimate friend of Merton, M. Basil Pennington wrote this book at Gethsemani Abbey where he lived in the hermitage where Merton spent his last five years. He offers an intimate glimpse of Merton's day-to-day living. With original photographs by Thomas Merton.

120 pages

M. Basil Pennington
THOMAS MERTON, BROTHER MONK
The Quest for True Freedom

"This is the Merton I knew—the seeker of God, the spiritual master. Each of the previous biographies has made its own unique contribution, but none has so explored the man's life. . . . A totally engaging and thoughtful work."

—James Finley

226 pages

At your bookstore or from the publisher:
The Continuum Publishing Company,
370 Lexington Avenue,
New York, NY 10017
1-800-561-7704